The Last Picture
Catherine Dyson

methuen | drama
LONDON • NEW YORK • OXFORD • NEW DELHI • SYDNEY

METHUEN DRAMA
Bloomsbury Publishing Plc, 50 Bedford Square, London, WC1B 3DP, UK
Bloomsbury Publishing Inc, 1359 Broadway, New York, NY 10018, USA
Bloomsbury Publishing Ireland, 29 Earlsfort Terrace, Dublin 2,
D02 AY28, Ireland

BLOOMSBURY, METHUEN DRAMA and the Methuen
Drama logo are trademarks of Bloomsbury Publishing Plc.

First published in Great Britain 2026

Copyright © Catherine Dyson, 2026

Catherine Dyson has asserted their right under the Copyright, Designs and Patents Act, 1988, to be identified as Author of this work.

Cover design: RachelO StudiO

All rights reserved. No part of this publication may be: i) reproduced or transmitted in any form, electronic or mechanical, including photocopying, recording or by means of any information storage or retrieval system without prior permission in writing from the publishers; or ii) used or reproduced in any way for the training, development or operation of artificial intelligence (AI) technologies, including generative AI technologies. The rights holders expressly reserve this publication from the text and data mining exception as per Article 4(3) of the Digital Single Market Directive (EU) 2019/790.

Bloomsbury Publishing Plc does not have any control over, or responsibility for, any third-party websites referred to or in this book. All internet addresses given in this book were correct at the time of going to press. The author and publisher regret any inconvenience caused if addresses have changed or sites have ceased to exist, but can accept no responsibility for any such changes.

No rights in incidental music or songs contained in the work are hereby granted and performance rights for any performance/presentation whatsoever must be obtained from the respective copyright owners.

All rights whatsoever in this play are strictly reserved and application for performance etc. should be made before rehearsals begin to United Agents12–26 Lexington Street, London, W1F 0LE.

No performance may be given unless a licence has been obtained.

A catalogue record for this book is available from the British Library.

Library of Congress Control Number: 2026930788

ISBN: PB: 978-1-3506-2300-2
ePDF: 978-1-3506-2301-9
eBook: 978-1-3506-2302-6

Series: Modern Plays

Typeset by Mark Heslington Ltd, Scarborough, North Yorkshire
Printed and bound in Great Britain

For product safety related questions contact
productsafety@bloomsbury.com.

To find out more about our authors and books visit
www.bloomsbury.com and sign up for our newsletters.

The Last Picture was first performed at York Theatre Royal on 5 February 2026.

A York Theatre Royal, ETT and An Tobar and Mull Production.

With **Robin Simpson** in the role of Sam.

Written by **Catherine Dyson**

Directed by **John R. Wilkinson**

Designed by **Natasha Jenkins**

Lighting Design by **Benny Goodman**

Sound Design by **Max Pappenheim**

Movement Direction by **Alexia Kalogiannidis**

Company Stage Manager **Sarah Goodyear**

Deputy Stage Manager **Jane Williamson**

Tour Deputy Stage Manager **Shay McCourt**

Tour Production Manager **Grace Duff**

With thanks to: Rebecca Atkinson-Lord, Jenny Bakst, Alessandro Bucci, Erin Carter, Gregory Clarke, Laura Crossley, Tim Crouch, Pippa Hill, Rebecca Latham, Rachel Mars, Madeleine O'Reilly, Jessy Roberts, Sam Thorpe-Spinks, Dr Elanor Stannage, Jessica Vaughan, Lilac Yosiphon, and the Peggy Ramsay Foundation.

The Last Picture was selected by the RSC in 2023 to be part of their 37 Plays national playwriting initiative.

Promotional Artwork and Cover Design by RachelO StudiO.

Tour Dates
York Theatre Royal 5–14 February 2026
HOME, Manchester 18–21 February 2026
Bristol Old Vic 24–28 February 2026
Yvonne Arnaud Theatre, Guildford 5–7 March 2026

ROBIN SIMPSON – SAM

Robin's recent theatre credits include: *Footloose, Beautiful: The Carole King Musical* and *Sense and Sensibility* at Pitlochry Festival Theatre.

Other theatre credits include: *Gaslight* and *Men of the World* as part of Devonshire Park Theatre's rep season; *Guy Fawkes* at York Theatre Royal; *Abigail's Party* at Harrogate Theatre and *Classic!* at the Edinburgh Fringe with Hope Mill Theatre/Her Productions. Robin played Benedick in Northern Broadsides' *Much Ado About Nothing* and toured nationally with *As You Like It*; *Macbeth/A Midsummer Night's Dream* (Shakespeare's Rose Theatre); *Dirty Laundry* (Claybody Theatre); *Anna of the Five Towns, Beryl, A Voyage Round My Father* and *Laurel and Hardy* (New Vic); *Chamaco*, (HOME, Manchester); *Neverland* (Lakeside Arts); *Boeing Boeing, Bedroom Farce, David Copperfield, The Hound of the Baskervilles, The Road to Nab End* and *Travels With My Aunt* (Oldham Coliseum); *The Travelling Pantomime, The Wind in the Willows, To Kill a Mockingbird, The Seagull, Hansel and Gretel, The Railway Children, Pinocchio, Pygmalion* and *The Little Mermaid* (York Theatre Royal); *Inside Out of Mind* (Meeting Ground Theatre Co.); *Grandpa in my Pocket* (Nottingham Playhouse); *Lost Boy Racer* (Lawrence Batley Theatre); *We Love You City!* (Coventry Belgrade); *Me, as a Penguin, It's a Lovely Day Tomorrow* and *Flat Stanley* (West Yorkshire Playhouse); *A Passionate Woman* (Chester Gateway and Theatre by the Lake); *Frankie and Tommy, The Rivals, Red Skies Over the Severn, The Century Plays* (The Swan Theatre).

Robin has played the Dame in York Theatre Royal's pantomimes since 2020 and is due to appear in *Snow White and the Seven Dwarfs* in 2026/27.

Television credits include: *The Continental: From the World of John Wick, Coronation Street, Emmerdale, Doctors, Holby City, Waterloo Road, Liverpool 1, Home Fires* and *See No Evil – The Moors Murders*.

CATHERINE DYSON – WRITER

Catherine Dyson is a writer and performer.

Her writing credits include: *The Luminous*, *On Track*, *Thunder Road* (RedCape Theatre, UK tours); *Peter Pan* (Sherman Theatre); *Bitcoin Boi* (Riverfront Theatre); *Believers* (South Street Arts Centre) and *Transporter* (Theatr Iolo, UK and Kolkata tour – also produced in Austria).

Writing credits for audio include: *The Egg Man* (BBC Radio 4) and *Mansfield Park* (eight-part adaptation for Audible).

She won second prize in the Arch 468 Hope Prize, has been shortlisted and specially commended in the Wales Writer in Residence Award and longlisted for the Funny Women Writing Award.

The Last Picture was selected as one of the RSC's 37 Plays in 2023. Catherine is an Associate Artist with RedCape Theatre and Theatr Iolo, and was a Resident Artist with Papertrail in 2025. She is currently on attachment with the National Theatre, and is a member of the Orange Tree Theatre's 2025/26 Writers Collective.

JOHN R. WILKINSON – DIRECTOR

John is a theatre director with quadriplegic cerebral palsy.

The Last Picture is his second collaboration with ETT and York Theatre Royal, following *Mugabe, My Dad and Me* by Tonderai Munyevu, which won Best New Play at the UK Theatre Awards 2022.

He received the Genesis Future Director's Award at the Young Vic, where he staged a sold-out production of *Winter* by Nobel laureate Jon Fosse. A 2024 Clore Fellow and member of Arts Council England's North Area Council, John also serves on the Boards of Middle Child, Pilot Theatre and Stephen Joseph Theatre in Scarborough.

From 2017 to 2019, he was Agent for Change at Leeds Playhouse and co-directed Alan Bennett's *Talking Heads*. As Associate

Director of York Theatre Royal, his credits include: *Sovereign*, *Hello and Goodbye*, *Swallows and Amazons* and *Can't Stand Up For Falling Down*.

John trained at Bretton Hall College and on the National Theatre Director's Course.

NATASHA JENKINS – DESIGNER

Theatre credits include: *Prendre Soin* (Théâtre National de Strasbourg); *Expendable* (Royal Court Theatre. Winner Best Stage Production Asian Media Awards 2025); *An Enemy of the People* (Duke of York's Theatre. Costume Designer); *LOVE* (National Theatre/Park Avenue Armory/Odéon-Théâtre de l'Europe/Wiener Festwochen. Nominated for Drama Desk Award for Outstanding Scenic Design); *Danton Reloaded* (Thalia Theater Hamburg. Costume Design); *The Beauty Queen of Leenane* (Theatre by the Lake); *The Process, Professor Bernhardi* (Theatre Freiburg. Costume Design); *Scissors* (Sheffield Theatres); *Une mort dans la famille* (Odéon-Théâtre de l'Europe); *Faith, Hope and Charity* (National Theatre/Wiener Festwochen/European tour); *Eine Griechische Trilogie* (Berliner Ensemble. Costume Design); *Beyond Caring* (National Theatre/The Yard/Schaubühne/European tour); *Uncle Vanya* (HOME, Manchester. Costume Design); *The High Table* (Bush Theatre); *In Basildon* (Queen's Theatre Hornchurch); *Richard III* (Perth Theatre); *Clockwork Canaries* (Drum Theatre Plymouth); *Stand By* (Utter. Fringe First Winner); *The Whip Hand* (National Theatre of Scotland/Traverse Theatre/Birmingham Rep); *Monstrous Bodies* (Dundee Rep); *20b* (Birmingham Rep/European tour); *Damned Rebel Bitches* (Poorboy Scottish tour); *Jane Eyre* (Guildhall); *Disney's Freaky Friday* (Arts Ed); *Romeo and Juliet* (RADA); *Let the Right One In* (LAMDA).

TV and film design credits include: *LOVE* (BBC1/Cuba Productions); *7 Keys* (Jeva Films SXSW '24); award winning short films including *BARE* and *Thursdays* (BFI Network, dir. Lorna Tucker); *A Sharp Arrow* (Sundance '23, dir. Sandy Thompson); *The Everlasting Club* and *Ma'am* (Bumble Female Film Force Winner 2019, dir. Joy Wilkinson); *Myrtle* and *Annekas Problems* (dir. Patricia

McCormack); *Loose Ends* (dir. Natalie Burt); *Forgiveness* (dir. Conor O'Callaghan); *Here We Are* (dir. Pamela Carter).

Music video design includes: *Anywhere But Here* (Rag'n'Bone Man and P!nk).

BENNY GOODMAN – LIGHTING DESIGNER

Benny Goodman is a freelance lighting designer based in Glasgow and London.

He has worked in theatres across the UK and Europe in a variety of projects and productions, and is a creative collaborator with theatre company, Wonder Fools.

Theatre credits include: *Close* (Citizens Theatre, Glasgow); *The Mountain Top* (The Royal Lyceum Theatre, Edinburgh); *Gods of Salford* (Not Too Tame/Lowry Theatre); *Treasure Island* (Scottish Theatre Producers); *Twelfth Night* (Shakespeare North); *Aganeeza Scrooge* (Tron Theatre); *Beauty and the Beast*, *Cinderella* and *Snow White* (Bard in the Botanics/Byre Theatre); *When Prophecy Fails* (Groupwork); *Four Walls* (Derby Theatre); *La Performance* (Tron Theatre/Paris IVT); *A Midsummer Night's Dream* (Orange Tree Theatre); *Hamlet* (Saint Stephen's Theatre); *Hang* (Tron Theatre); *Sense of Centre* (Dance Base Edinburgh); *Julius Caesar* (Company of Wolves Scottish tour); *Palace of Varieties* (Derby Theatre); *Learning from the Future* (OGR Torino); *The Tempest* (Tron Theatre); *Meet Jan Black* (Ayr Gaiety); *Maim* (Tron Theatre); *I Can Go Anywhere* (Traverse Theatre); *The Drift* (National Theatre of Scotland); *The Afflicted* (Summerhall); *Country Music* (Omnibus Theatre); *549: Scots of the Spanish Civil War* (UK tour); *The Mistress Contract* (Tron Theatre); *Daddy Drag* (Assembly Roxy); *Where We Are: The Mosque* (Arcola Theatre, London); *Sorella Mia* (The Place, London); *Disarming Reverberations* (St Giles' Cathedral, Edinburgh); *Heroines* (Theatre Gu Leor, Stornoway); *Humbug* (Tramway, Glasgow); *Snow Queen* (Associate – Dundee Rep Theatre); *Like Animals* (Tron Theatre); *Ayanfe Opera* (Bridewell Theatre, London); *Lampedusa* (Citizens Theatre); *Circle of Fifths* (Tron Theatre/Cockpit Theatre, London).

For more on his work: bennygoodman.co

MAX PAPPENHEIM – SOUND DESIGNER

Recent theatre credits include: *Christmas Day* (Almeida Theatre); *The Forsyte Saga* (Royal Shakespeare Company/Park Theatre); *Noughts and Crosses*, *Twelfth Night* (Regent's Park Open Air Theatre); *A Raisin in the Sun* (Headlong); *The Night of the Iguana* (Noel Coward Theatre); *The School for Scandal, Crooked Dances* (Royal Shakespeare Company); *Cruise* (Apollo Theatre/Duchess Theatre); *Coram Boy, Macbeth* (Chichester Festival Theatre); *Shed: Exploded View* (Royal Exchange); *A Doll's House Part 2, The Way of the World* (Donmar Warehouse); *The Cardinal, Kiki's Delivery Service, Usagi Yojimbo, Johnny Got His Gun, Teddy* (Southwark Playhouse); *Personal Values, The Habits, The Invention of Love, King James, Nineteen Gardens, Blackout Songs, Linck and Mülhahn, Labyrinth* (Hampstead Theatre); *The Children* (Manhattan Theatre Club/Royal Court); *Village Idiot, One Night in Miami* (Nottingham Playhouse); *Henry V* (Shakespeare's Globe/Headlong); *Hamlet* (Bristol Old Vic); *Ophelias Zimmer* (Schaubühne/Royal Court); *Feeling Afraid as if Something Terrible is Going to Happen, Old Bridge* (Bush Theatre); *The Homecoming, My Cousin Rachel* (Theatre Royal, Bath); *Playhouse Creatures, Churchill in Moscow, Humble Boy, Blue/Heart, The Distance* (Orange Tree Theatre); *Single White Female, Picture You Dead, Art, The Syndicate, Murder in the Dark, The Mirror Crack'd, Wish You Were Dead, The Circle, Looking Good Dead* (national tours).

Opera and ballet credits include: *Kirsten Flagstad* (Bergen International Festival); *The Limit* (Royal Ballet); *The Marriage of Figaro* (Salzburg Festival); *Miranda* (Opéra Comique, Paris); *Hansel and Gretel* (BYO/Opera Holland Park); *Scraww* (Trebah Gardens).

Online includes: *The System, Barnes' People, The Haunting of Alice Bowles* (Original Theatre); *15 Heroines* (Digital Theatre).

Max is an associate artist of Orange Tree Theatre, The Faction and Silent Opera.

Awards include Off West End Award for Sound Design for *Old Bridge*.

ALEXIA KALOGIANNIDIS – MOVEMENT DIRECTOR

Alexia Kalogiannidis is a movement artist who works across movement direction, choreography, movement research and performance. Her practice centres on physical storytelling, character embodiment and close observation of human behaviour. She is interested in how detailed physicality and intentional movement shape the audience's experience by influencing the often subconscious, visual information they interpret from the body on stage.

Alexia works collaboratively with directors and performers to explore how movement can reveal relationships, inner worlds and unspoken tensions within a narrative. Drawing from a wide range of movement practices and embodied research, she develops physical languages that are responsive to text, atmosphere and the human dynamics at the heart of a production.

She trained at London Contemporary Dance School and then went on to completing a Masters at Northern School of Contemporary Dance. Since graduating, she has worked as a freelance movement artist across the UK and Europe, contributing to projects in film, theatre, photography and visual art.

SARAH GOODYEAR – COMPANY STAGE MANAGER

Sarah trained in Production Arts (Stage Management, Lighting and Sound) at Liverpool Community College. Her stage management experience is long and varied.

Credits include: *Steel* (Theatre by the Lake); *Mary and The Hyenas* (Hull Truck Theatre); *Baby, He Loves You* (Middle Child Theatre); *Invisible Cities* (Manchester International Festival and Brisbane Festival); *A Streetcar Named Desire* (Royal Exchange Theatre); *The Last Testament of Lillian Bilocca* (Hull Capital of Culture); *The Last Days of Troy* (Shakespeare's Globe Theatre).

JANE WILLIAMSON – DEPUTY STAGE MANAGER

Jane has worked as a Stage Manager for over ten years. For most of her career she has worked as a Deputy Stage Manager for, among other theatres and theatre companies, Hull Truck Theatre, York Theatre Royal, Stephen Joseph Theatre and the Young Vic. Jane also works as Company Manager for Next Door But One.

SHAY MCCOURT – TOUR DEPUTY STAGE MANAGER

Shay studied Stage Management and Technical Production at the Edinburgh School of Stage Management, graduating in 2023.

They have worked on plays, new musicals and tours, filling a variety of stage management and technical roles.

Theatre credits include: *Jack and the Beanstalk: a New Moosical* (Dundee Rep Theatre); *Pirates!* (Scottish Dance Theatre); *All Will Be Well* (Dundee Rep Theatre); *Wild Rose* (Royal Lyceum Theatre, Edinburgh, Gavin Kalin Productions, Caledonia Productions); *Sleeping Beauty* (Imagine Theatre, OnFife); *Anna Hibiscus' Song* (Utopia Theatre); *Wake Up* (Solar Bear); *The Wonderful Wizard of Oz* (Theatre Royal, Bury St Edmunds); *Cloud Man* (Constellation Points, Theatre in Schools Scotland); *The Little Mermaid* (Imagine Theatre, OnFife); *Who Killed My Father* (surrogate.); *The Multiverse is Gay!* (Royal Lyceum Theatre, Edinburgh); *Macbeth* (An Undoing) (Royal Lyceum Theatre, Edinburgh); *Cinderella* (Imagine Theatre, OnFife); *Rocket Post* (Constellation Points).

YORK THEATRE ROYAL

For more than 280 years, York Theatre Royal has welcomed and entertained the people of York, offering a diverse programme for audiences of all ages to enjoy.

With the support of Arts Council England, and working alongside creative partners, York Theatre Royal is continually building on its reputation for producing high quality ambitious theatre. As well as creating exciting new work, with and for its community in York, its aspiration is also to build national and international relationships to take its work to other parts of the UK and across the globe.

York Theatre Royal has one of the best auditoriums for dance and is proud to welcome national and internationally renowned dance companies giving audiences the chance to see innovative world-class dance, in York.

The theatre's curated programme of presented work also offers audiences opportunities to see Olivier-award winning shows, West End productions and new work from innovative touring companies and local artists. Stand-up, drama, comedy, music, family shows and more are on offer in the theatre's diverse programme of presented work.

Community is at the heart of York Theatre Royal. Its work within local communities is an essential part of what it does, and it is proud of its proactive creative engagement programme which reaches people from a wide variety of different backgrounds and ages. Ensuring arts and culture is accessible to all, is vital. York Theatre Royal will always be a local theatre and creative hub which is here for its community.

yorktheatreroyal.co.uk

ETT

'English, Touring and Theatre are my three favourite words in the English language. Put together they are more wonderful still.' Sir Ian McKellen, ETT Patron.

Over the past thirty-two years, ETT has toured 115 productions to 107 towns and cities all over the world, seen by over 2.1 million audience members, presented in 142 theatres.

ETT (English Touring Theatre) is a UK-based international touring company. It stages both new and classic productions of outstanding quality, imagination and ambition; interrogating and celebrating contemporary England; sparking national and global conversations. You can find ETT's work in your local theatre, online, at festivals, internationally and in the West End.

ETT believes in the power of creative collaboration, and works in partnership with visionary artists and venues. It believes that touring is a democratic and imaginative way to meet audiences and communities in their hometowns and cities, storytelling on a national canvas.

ETT has won the UK Theatre Awards Best Touring Production in 2014, 2015, 2016, Best Play Revival in 2019, Excellence in Inclusivity and Best New Play in 2022, and Excellence in Touring in 2023. Founded in 1993, ETT is a limited company and a registered charity, based in London.

To find out how you can support ETT please go to ett.org.uk/support

AN TOBAR AND MULL THEATRE

An Tobar and Mull Theatre is a multi-artform creative powerhouse nestled on the wild, sea-lashed edge of Scotland. Based in the Hebrides on the Isle of Mull, it makes and shares brave, generous, beautifully-crafted art that's born of difficult questions, not easy answers. It champions the voices of islanders, Gaels, dreamers, doers and artists of all kinds – and it tells stories that ripple out from its shores into the wider world. It is the only producing theatre in the Hebrides, but it is far more than a theatre. It's a gallery, a music venue, a community resource, a space for discovery and delight. It is the cultural beating heart of its island – a place where artists and audiences gather, connect and make something extraordinary together.

An Tobar and Mull Theatre believes in art that matters – made with care, curiosity and joy – and it supports artists at every stage of their journey, offering residencies, commissions, mentoring, and a strong cup of tea. Its buildings are a lighthouse and a hearth: a place to gather and a place to find your way home. Each year, An Tobar and Mull Theatre produces and tours bold new work, presents a rich programme of live events, exhibitions and film, and delivers creative learning for every school child on the island. It hosts music from ceilidh to contemporary, dance for toddlers to elders, and everything in between. Its audience is fiercely local and joyfully global – connected by a shared sense of wonder.

antobarandmulltheatre.co.uk

WRITER'S NOTE

In 1939, my grandfather left his home in Poland and crossed the Tatra Mountains alone, on foot, with a single suitcase. In the suitcase was a bundle of photographs of people of all ages – family, friends, his fiancée – that he left behind. Most of the people in the photographs were murdered, many names and identities now lost. In one of these pictures, my grandfather walks down a tree-lined street, arms linked with his fiancée, both of them smiling into the camera, radiating happiness and love.

A photograph doesn't explain anything. All it can say is: this was us, we existed in this moment. Looking at a picture of a Jewish child in a ghetto in 1943, or a Palestinian mother amongst the rubble of her home in 2025, does not explain why these things happen and keep happening.

But if we picture ourselves – human beings – with honesty and compassion, we must acknowledge our capacity for destruction and hatred, as well as for kindness, beauty and love. We are all of us all of these things, and we are at each other's mercy.

I hope that this play offers you courage, to look at all of the pictures all around us.

The young couple arm in arm beneath the trees.

The mother in the rubble.

A dog running with a group of children through a sunlit field, barking with spontaneous, unbridled joy.

Catherine Dyson

DIRECTOR'S NOTE

Making *The Last Picture* has been a rare challenge. It's one that asks the actor, creative team and audience alike to stretch their imaginations. This production invites you to consciously co-create the piece. Your imagination isn't an optional layer; it's part of the performance's architecture. What happens onstage and what you build in your mind meet to complete the world of the play.

To support this, I draw your attention to Peak Mind's exercise *Finding Your Flashlight*: your attention is a beam, and where you direct it shapes your experience. It encourages deep imagining, sustained focus and empathy. Throughout the performance, you're asked to illuminate not only what you see but also the emotional and symbolic spaces that remain unseen. When your attention becomes deliberate, you become an active participant in the story.

This suits *The Last Picture* particularly well. Catherine's play begins in symbolism and shifts gradually toward realism, a journey we've tried to honour in our staging. Early images are loose and poetic, becoming more grounded as the world steadies into something recognisable. Symbolism asks for intuitive seeing; realism asks for understanding. That movement comes fully alive only through collective attention.

We make this production at a moment when the world feels anything but symbolic. Ongoing suffering forms part of the emotional landscape into which the play arrives. While it doesn't address current events, it resonates against a backdrop where empathy feels both urgent and fragile. Theatre can't solve conflicts, but it can remind us how to hold complex humanity in our minds. It can rehearse compassion.

My thanks go to the extraordinary creative team whose commitment and imagination shape every moment. Their work invites you to look closely, think freely, and feel bravely.

So today or tonight, I ask only this: Use your imagination. Let it meet ours. And enjoy the show.

Woof!

John R. Wilkinson

The Last Picture

Notes

This is a play for one voice, for an actor of any age, gender or ethnicity.

The performer should always address the audience.

The play is set in the present.

The pictures that are described by the performer should not be represented visually in any way – they are constructed in the imaginations of performer and audience.

All of the pictures described are real.

Good evening.
Thank you for coming.
How is everybody feeling?

First things first –
A head count.

A head count.

This and subsequent head counts should acknowledge the actual number of people in the room at the time.

Good.
There are ___ of us.

Let me introduce myself
I will be your companion for the evening
My name is Sam
I am a dog.
I've got a patchy coat
A bit scraggly
Different shades of brown and white
I've got a small scar on my muzzle
Just below my left eye
(Which is a different colour to my right eye).
I'm no pedigree.
I have no idea of my heritage
Of the purity
Or impurity
Of my line.
I suppose I'm what you would call
A mongrel.
Nevertheless
I'd like to assure you
That I'm a professional.
I am here to look after you.
You're in good hands with me.
I'm not any old mutt

4 The Last Picture

I'm a specialist.
I've got a certificate
And a uniform
To prove it
I'm an emotional support dog.
I can alleviate your anxiety
Ease your sadness
Calm your fears.
I can steady your breathing
Lower your blood pressure
It's a fact.
When your feelings threaten to overwhelm you
I can carry them for you.
There's an unprecedented demand right now
For animals like me.
Because
It seems
These days
You're feeling somewhat shaky
You feel
The sands shift beneath your feet
And outside your door
A storm rages.
It's hard sometimes
To hold it together
To face it
To keep going.

I had an intensive training.
It taught me to be attuned to your feelings
To recognise signs of discomfort and distress
To help you through
The white shock of the days
And the long dark hours of the nights
To always be there
With a look
A lick
I was even taught how

If your heart races
Your breath catches
You feel like you're losing yourself
To use my body weight
To bring you back to yourself
By lying on your chest
Or across your lap.
It's called
Deep Pressure Therapy
You can look it up.
It really works.

Are you feeling okay so far?

Okay
So
Before we begin
Something else my training has taught me is
That it's important for you
To know where you are
Who you are
And what is going on
At all times.
Don't worry
I will keep letting you know.
Right now
We are in a theatre.
You are you
– People,
Human beings –
I am a dog.

We are here to witness a story.
We are all in this story.
This story is told in pictures.
It is important that we look at them.
Some of them are huge and fill up the whole space
Some of them are very small and require you to look closely.

6 The Last Picture

You might be surprised to find that sometimes
You can quite comfortably take in the very large pictures
While the small ones can be intense and overwhelming.
Some of the pictures are beautiful
Some of them are boring
Some of them are upsetting.
It's not always possible to know which pictures you will find beautiful, boring or upsetting
Until you really look at them.
Sometimes the description of the picture is more disturbing than the actual picture itself.

I won't be affected by the pictures
They won't touch me
Because as a dog
I cannot, unlike your good selves
Have a sophisticated understanding of what's going on in the images.
I don't have a concept of things such as
Morality
Injustice
Or conscience.
But
As I'm sure you know
All dogs are sensitive to human emotions
And even specialist training aside
I can see how you are feeling
Literally
In full and vivid colour.

I will be receiving those emotions
Absorbing them
Without having to deal with
The context
The history
The messy human-ness of it all.
And while you, at times,
May not always feel yourselves,

Throughout this evening
I will always be
Sam the dog.

About the colours I mentioned.
It's a commonly held misconception
That dogs can't see colours
Yes, it's true that we have an acute sense of smell
But there's more to us than our noses
Sometimes you humans know less than you think.
I can see a full spectrum of colours,
Just not the same ones as you
So, if, for example
I tell you now
That you are radiating
A wash of emerald green
With pulses of indigo
The colours that you picture
Won't be the same as those I see.

Some final housekeeping:
You are free to leave at any time.
The doors are open
An usher will assist you.
Please feel at liberty to eat and drink.
It is okay
To talk quietly
To move around
If you need to
But please try to pay attention
Please try to look at the pictures
And listen to the story
If you can.
Thank you.
Any questions?
Shall we begin?

*

8 The Last Picture

Let's look at the first picture.
This is a picture of you and me.
You are a class of schoolchildren
Year 9
You're thirteen, fourteen years old.
You're in your uniforms
Dark blue blazer with a yellow and blue striped tie.
You're standing in the yard in front of your school
Holding a banner saying
Welcome Sam!
You're smiling
You're transmitting a shade of pale amber.
You're gathered around me
Jostling to be near me
My tail is a blur
I'm wearing a hi-vis harness which says
Emotional Support Animal.
I'm standing at your feet
Looking straight at the camera.
The person behind the camera is Sir.
So he is not in this picture.

Here is a picture of Sir
From the staff page on the school website.
Perhaps he's in his early forties
Clean shaven
His hair is greying at the temples
He's trying to smile but it's not quite registering.
He looks a bit stiff
A bit uncomfortable in the shirt and tie
He probably wears jeans at home
Maybe he's into some of the same bands as you
Perhaps he's even got one or two tattoos.
He's got an intense aura of ultramarine about him.
The description says that Sir
'Is Head of History and a passionate advocate for pupil wellbeing.'

Let's go back to that first picture for a moment
The one of us together in the school yard.
Sir is explaining
That in my role as Year 9 emotional support dog
I will be a permanent member of our class
I will provide comfort and companionship
I will alleviate stress and sensory overload.
Some of you want to know how I'm going to do that
It's just a dog, Sir
Not a psychologist
Some of you have questions
About whether I can open doors, predict thunderstorms, or do maths
(Answer: none of the above)
One of you has seen a thing on YouTube called
Fake Support Animals Wreak Havoc!
In the film
A woman takes a chinchilla out of her handbag on a plane
Forcing the pilot to make an emergency landing
A pot bellied pig runs amok in an art gallery
And a man tries to get a table at a Michelin star restaurant
with a python draped around his neck
Terrifying the other diners.
Sir says no, it's nothing like that
This dog is properly trained and certified
Fully licensed
And has supreme self control.
Sir describes
How part of my training
Involved learning to walk past a whole roast chicken
Without twitching a nose muscle
How I had to stand stock still
Not bat an eyelid
While a ball arced gloriously behind my head
Sir watches you pet and pat me
He hopes he's done the right thing
It's been a battle to get management on side
To agree to having an animal in the school

10 The Last Picture

But he pushed for it
Because the truth is
Sir worries about you.
It's been a difficult time
And the world is a frightening place
He has noticed that lately
That you seem a bit all over the shop
Distracted
Emotional
Only that morning
He has had to keep some of you behind after class
To ask about a video you were sharing
Of a real life execution
And at break time
A few of you found a baby bird that had fallen to its death from a nest
You were inconsolable.
Sir thinks
That in some ways you seem very old and careworn
Cynical even
Like you've seen it all
And in other ways
Very sensitive and fragile.
None of that really comes across in the picture, but
Do you recognise that description of yourselves at all?

This is a picture of a book with a man on the cover
Beard and glasses
A worried expression on his face
Sir posts it on the classroom app
It's a story set in 1930s Poland
About a Jewish doctor who ran an orphanage.
It's a novel
But it's based on fact.
Sir recommends the book
He has observed that there are some gaps in your knowledge
Of European history

There's been a recent incident
That began with
A swastika drawn on someone's locker
Sir wonders if you even know what that represents
Really?
He hoped the whole thing would blow over
But it escalated
The parents got involved
It turned really nasty
A couple of kids were scared to come to school
And some of the families still aren't speaking to each other.

Sir is planning a trip to an exhibition
Details TBC.

Is everyone okay?
Is anyone feeling sick?

You are a class of Year 9 schoolchildren
We are not in a school yard any more
We're on a bus
Travelling down a motorway
This is a picture of you on the bus
Some of you have put on a bit of makeup
Worn your favourite trainers
Made an effort with your hair
Because we're going on a trip and you want to look your best.

You shimmer with shades of orange
Tangerine and marigold and tortoiseshell
Throwing out little sparks into the air as you move.

Some of you have gone a bit overboard with the snacks and fizzy drinks
Some of you are feeling a bit nauseous
The windows have been opened for ventilation
One of you is asleep.

12 The Last Picture

Some of you
The ones at the back
Are up to all sorts
Through the rear window
Trying to get a reaction from other drivers
I'm sitting up the front with Sir
He's drinking coffee and biting his nails
He's hoping that this is the right thing to do.
That it won't be too much for you.
He has studied the website carefully
He has read every word of the sensitive content guide
He's glad that I'm here
It's clear that you've become attached to me
That you feel more secure with me around.
I'm looking out the window
With my tongue lolling out
Watching the empty fields and distant towns go past
A bird of prey hovers then plummets
I don't know where we are any more
I wonder where we're going.

This is a picture that one of you took of the car park when we arrived.
There's not much to say about this picture
A line of buses
Anonymous people getting off them
Bleary eyed
A little disorientated
Sputtering weak rays of malachite
You know that feeling
When after a long journey
You arrive in an unknown place?

Head count!

A head count.

It's vital that no one gets been left behind.

The Last Picture

Sir reminds you of the rules
That you must stay with the group at all times
That phones must be switched off and kept out of sight
He reminds you that you are representing the school
That he expects the highest standard of behaviour from you.
Do you have any questions?
You want to know where the toilets are
You want to know if you should bring your bags
You want to know when you'll eat

You are a class of Year 9 schoolchildren
You are not on the bus anymore
You are inside a museum.
Here is a picture
That one of you took of me
Waiting patiently at the ticket desk
While Sir explains the presence of a dog in the museum to the staff
And shows the required paperwork.
In the picture
You can see the patches of sweat on Sir's shirt
He's generating agitated pulses of citrine yellow
He turns around and snaps at you
Have you got a two minute memory or what
Put that phone *away*.

You are still the class of Year 9 schoolchildren.
I am still Sam the dog.
We are about to enter an exhibition.
These next pictures,
They're all in black and white.
They aren't ours
They are other people's pictures
Please pay attention.

Is everybody okay?
It's essential that we all stay together.

14 The Last Picture

Let's go in.

A sign at the entrance says:
'This exhibition is not recommended for children under the age of 14.'
Some of you nudge each other
Because there are a few of you
The ones who have late summer birthdays
Who are still thirteen.

We are in the first room of the exhibition.
There is a big sign saying
'Before.'
There are lots of pictures in this room.
Life size
Portraits of people
With their names
And a bit about their lives
Who they were and what they hoped for
There are smaller pictures
Groups of people
Seaside holidays
Picnics by lakes
Friends in back gardens
Family reunions
Ice skating
School concerts . . .
I think maybe these pictures bore you a little bit
Perhaps you don't understand why you are looking at them.
You shuffle your feet
And shift your backpacks
Sir notices that one of you is chewing gum
He tells you to put it in the bin
He says it's disrespectful.
He says
Look at these pictures
There are a lot of kids your age in them

The Last Picture

Please look
They're just like you.

One of you notices a picture
Of a little curly-haired boy
Sitting on a park bench
With his arms around a dog
You say
That dog looks just like Sam
And Sir says
You're right
Spitting image
Doppelgänger
Some of you lift me up to get a better look
I wag my tail furiously
But then people are staring at us
We're attracting too much attention
And Sir says
Put the dog down for goodness sake
Jets of vermilion fill the air
Like smoke signals
And the moment passes.

You are still a class of Year 9 schoolchildren.
I am still Sam the dog.
We are moving into the next room of the exhibition.
In this room
There are many pictures of a man
The same man
The same face
Here he is kissing a little girl who is presenting him with a bunch of flowers
Here he is standing on a platform addressing a crowd of thousands
Here he is staring intensely into the camera
Like a movie star
You recognise this man
You haven't been living under a rock or something

16 The Last Picture

You know who he is
You have an idea of what he did
What he represents
You know
That when people want to describe the worst of humanity
They reach for his name
But all the same
It's just a man
In one sense he could be any man
And after you've seen his face a few times
A haze fills the room
The colour of coral
And you start to glaze over a bit.
Perhaps you're feeling a bit hungry
Wondering if we'll get ice cream later
Or if we'll stop at a services on the way home
There's a Burger King in the one near junction 28 on the M4
And your dad gave you a fiver for the trip.
Perhaps you're wondering what we are doing here
Why we came all this way
To look at this stuff.

Sir gathers you around
He directs you to a picture of a group of young people in uniform
Sitting round a campfire
He explains
It was kind of like the scouts
It was a way of indoctrinating young people
Some of you think it looks fun
Some of you think you wouldn't be seen dead in a group like that
You keeping looking at this picture
Imagining the scene

And

For a brief moment
You are not you, the audience in a theatre.

You are not the class of Year 9 schoolchildren in a museum

You are a group of teenagers
Sitting in a field at dusk
Almost a century ago
Your cheeks flushed from the heat of the bonfire
The scent of the dark pine forest behind you
You are being told that you are important
That you are the future
The best of us
You are going to be called upon to defend your way of life and your identity
To stand together and fight for your place in the world
Are you up to it?

Now you are once again the class of Year 9 schoolchildren
We are back in the museum together.

We are looking at another picture.
It is a picture of a family called
The Ideal Family
They are white skinned and blond haired
They aren't real
It's a painting.
A broad chested father
A gentle, smiling mother cradling a baby
A blue-eyed boy and girl
A sleek, wolf-like dog lying at their feet

Perhaps you are thinking
That doesn't look like my family
My family looks nothing like that at all.

That dog in that picture
There's something about him that makes me nervous

18 The Last Picture

Maybe I let out a little whimper
A tiny whine
Because suddenly
I feel your hands reaching down
And gently patting my head.

This next picture is a kind of chart
It's pictures of people
Who don't look like
The Ideal Family
People with different shades of skin
Different shapes of faces
Different kinds of hair
These are not paintings
These are photographs of real human beings
Perhaps when you are looking at this picture
These faces meeting your gaze
Some of you recognise yourselves.

Sir has noticed that some of you have become thoughtful
He asks

Is everyone okay?

You are still the class of Year 9 schoolchildren.
We are still in the exhibition.
I am still Sam the emotional support dog.
Here is the next picture.
It's quite small
About the size of an A5 piece of paper
You have to get close to see what is going on.
Come a bit nearer.
In this picture, a dark haired woman is flanked by two men
in suits and smart wool coats
They are in a meadow on a bright sunny day
The sky is blue
The trunks of silver birches shine in the background
The woman is wearing a pink striped blouse

One of her sleeves is pushed up above her elbow
The man on the right smiles down at her as he holds a
needle to her vein
As if he is her family doctor
Reassuring her
That this is for her own good
The man on the left holds a cloth
And a small vial at the ready
His expression is unreadable.
There is nothing ambiguous about the woman's expression.
She is afraid.

Sir reads out the caption next to the picture:
'A doctor takes a blood sample from a Roma woman as part
of Nazi research into eugenics.'

There is another man in the foreground wearing a leather
jacket
He is looking at the woman
His back to the camera
You wonder who he is
Her husband perhaps
Or her son.

Sir is explaining the meaning of eugenics
But you're not paying attention to him
Because

For a moment, you are no longer the audience in the theatre
Or the class of Year 9 schoolchildren in the museum
You are the man in the leather jacket in the meadow in 1938
You are turning towards this woman
Who could be your wife
Your sister
Your mother
Your cousin
Your friend
You look on

20 The Last Picture

Paralysed
Like in a scene from a nightmare.

You are the class of Year 9 schoolchildren again
You are back in the exhibition.
You draw away from the picture
Perhaps you feel disturbed
Perhaps you feel confused
A feeling like watching the start of a forbidden horror film
In the middle of the day
With the sunlight streaming in through the open window.

Your eyes search for something else
Something ordinary
Something less frightening . . .
Here is a picture of a paper with numbered questions
Like a multiple choice test in school
The answers have been marked with ticks and crosses
There are many more crosses than ticks
It's the IQ test of a fifteen-year-old girl called Erika
It makes you sweat just looking at it
You're thinking about the school hall when it's set up for exams
How none of the techniques seem to work
The deep breathing
The relaxation exercises
The picturing of a positive outcome.
Your mind goes blank as soon as you turn over the paper
You feel like you couldn't answer the questions if your life depended on it
Perhaps Erika's mind went blank too
Because she got a very bad score
A score that meant she was considered unfit for education
They reckoned it was not worth the cost
To the hard-working taxpayer
And she was put in a special institution
But of course that is also expensive
And ultimately the sums just didn't add up

The books did not balance
So

Here is a picture of a van
Like the school minibus but with the windows papered over
And one day
A few months after Erika took that IQ test
She was taken away somewhere in a van like this
And her death was recorded neatly on a form.

Sir is looking intently at the picture
His mouth a tight line
One of you asks what eugenics is
And he says
I just explained that
You should have been listening.
Pulses of persimmon rise into the air like fireflies.

Time for a head count.

A head count.

Are you feeling alright?
Perhaps you'd like a sip of water
It's warm in here
I'll ask if it's possible to open a window.

You are the class of Year 9 schoolchildren
I am Sam the dog
We carry on moving through the exhibition
You are radiating pure sky blue.
Perhaps you're drifting off a little
Perhaps your minds are wandering
Sir is saying something about swimming
You're thinking about how it would be nice to go swimming
On a hot day like this
There's a spot in the river that flows through the park
Where everyone goes in the summer

22 The Last Picture

There's a little cafe selling cold drinks
Branches overhang the water
You can drift on your back
Watching the clouds move slowly high above you
If you're feeling brave
You can jump from the bridge into the deep part of the river
I chase sticks carried by the current
Shake my fur dry on the bank
But Sir is saying
Look
Look at this picture
The sign on the river bank:
'No entry for Dogs or Jews.'
There are other pictures of signs in this room
There are signs everywhere you turn
'Jews are not wanted in our district'
'Jews are not welcome'
'No service for Jews'
'No prescriptions for Jews'
'Aryans only'
'This is an Aryan town.'

We are moving into the next room of the exhibition.
This room is full of pictures of destruction
There are shops with smashed windows
There are burning buildings
Sir is explaining
That the devastation in these pictures took place
On a night in November 1938
He is telling you that
Thousands of synagogues were burned to the ground
Thousands of Jewish homes and businesses destroyed
The sound of windows smashing could be heard across the country
They called it Kristallnacht
The Night of Broken Glass
Sir is trying to convey the scale of destruction
The personal impact on individuals

The Last Picture

He knows that some of you
Have parents who run their own businesses
Imagine
Sir says
If your dad's shop was smashed up
If your mum's salon was set fire to.
But why would anybody do that?
You can't imagine it
It wouldn't happen.
It's depressing looking at all these pictures of broken things
There's too much to be sad about as it is
You start to pull away
But Sir says
Wait
Look at this
Look at this one.

In this picture
Three men in uniform are wrecking someone's house
A room with heavy furniture and patterned wallpaper
One of you is thinking it looks a bit like your nana's dining room
A man is pulling books from a bookshelf and chucking them on the floor
Another is breaking a dining chair
The third is tipping out the contents of some drawers
He is smoking a cigarette as he bends over them
Like what he's doing is no big deal
The rug is littered with papers and broken furniture
In the corner of the room is an overturned table
There is a fourth man at the edge of the picture
A young man not much older than you
One of you is thinking that he looks a bit like your cousin Darryl
You can just about make out the skull and crossbones on his hat
If you lean in really close.
He is gesturing to someone behind him

24 The Last Picture

As if he is telling them to
Get in the other room
Or
Calm down
Or
Keep that kid quiet
Or perhaps he is telling the person behind the camera not to take the photo
But the photo was taken
And here we are looking at it right now
In a theatre in 2026.

For a minute
You are not the audience in the theatre
Or the class of Year 9 schoolchildren in the museum.
You are the citizens of a German city
On the night of the ninth of November 1938.
You have heard rumours that there's going to be trouble tonight
That means different things depending on who you are
You are the next door neighbours
Of the people who live in the home in the picture
Perhaps you have decided
That the best course of action is to keep a low profile
These are frightening times
For everyone.
You stay inside your apartment
You have no intention of participating
In whatever might unfold tonight
You're not thugs.
You're in your dressing gowns when
You hear shouting from next door
A terrible commotion
The sound of stuff being thrown around
The baby screaming
The dog barking
A voice yelling:
Shut that fucking dog up!

The Last Picture

You look at each other.
You should do something.
Should you do something?

You've no quarrel with your neighbours
They're a quiet, polite family
Not that you really know them
You've only been in there once
Late summer, a few years back
Their first child had just been born
And you went round with a gift
But
These are different times
Difficult days
It's hard to know what to think at the moment.
You hear a woman's voice pleading
One of you cautiously ventures outside
You peer into the corridor and ask a man in uniform
What in Christ's name is going on in there
He tells you to
Get back inside.

What can you do?
You tried.
Sort of.
Better just brush your teeth and go to bed.
The racket goes on into the early hours
None of you get a wink of sleep
It's not just next door
It's all around.
When one of you gets up and peeks out the window
There are things being flung out into the streets
From the buildings opposite
Chairs
Beds
Pot plants
Plates
Pianos . . .

26 The Last Picture

In the days to come
You will hear stories of
How beloved pets were thrown from windows too
That can't be true
Can it?
They say that Jewish men were beaten in the streets
Arrested
And taken away from their families
To who knows where.
You think
It's hard to know what to believe
People do like to exaggerate
And anyway
It's not really any of your business
You've got your own troubles.
Next door have been quiet since
You haven't heard the baby cry
Or the dog bark
And when you walk by their apartment on your way out to the shops a few days later
The door's ajar
You push it open
The apartment is empty
Your neighbours have gone.

Are you all still with me?

A head count.

Soon we will have a break maybe
An intermission
Perhaps Sir will take us outside for some fresh air
We will bring up the house lights a little
And play some gentle music
Soon.
But for the time being
You are not in the theatre
Or the exhibition

The Last Picture

You are still the citizens of a German city.
Mannheim, 1941.

Here is the next picture.
It's a flyer that comes through your letterbox
An advert for an auction
It's a bit faded now
There are lines across it
From where you folded it into quarters
And put it in your back pocket
While you thought about whether you would go along.
On the leaflet
Is a picture of a well-furnished room
Not that different to the one in the previous picture.
But in this room,
All is in order
The books are on the shelves
The furniture is in its place
The curtains are drawn open to let the sunlight in.
Everything in this house is for sale
The leaflet says
Furniture
Crockery
Pots and pans
Books and bedding
Toys and clothes
There's an address
A date and a time
And some helpful information about bus routes.
And in small print at the bottom:
'Household items from non-Aryan property.'
You study the picture
Keep taking it out of your pocket to have another look
There's some good stuff there.
That's a nice lamp.
You could do with a good lamp.
You've heard about these auctions
They're happening all over the city

28 The Last Picture

Some of your friends have been
And picked up a bargain.
Perhaps you don't read the small print
Perhaps you don't understand it
Anyway,
There's no harm in going along
And just having a look
Is there?

Inside the apartment
It's clean and tidy
Apart from
A used coffee cup on the draining board
A dog bowl full of kibble next to the fridge
A pair of stockings hung up to dry in the bathroom
Five toothbrushes left in the cup by the basin
It's a bit odd if you stop to think about it
(Which you can't, you're in a hurry trying to get round and see everything)
In a child's bedroom
There are toys scattered on the floor
As if they had been forced to abandon their play.
Quite a few people have turned up
The auctioneer is pleased
A good turnout
Some of you exchange friendly chit chat
And light hearted banter
About having your eyes on the same items
You end up bidding on a few things
You come away with that lamp you wanted
A couple of paintings
A lovely tea set
And a carved dark wood sideboard.
You're glad you went along actually
It was a snip
Peanuts really for that lot
With free delivery thrown in –
It'll be a job to get that heavy sideboard up the stairs.

The Last Picture

If you wonder at all who this stuff belongs to
Who lived here
And where they might have gone
You don't dwell on it.
It seems unlikely that they're coming back.
You come out onto the street
Blinking in the bright winter light.

You are the class of Year 9 schoolchildren in the museum.
You are gleaming like dull silver.

Sir is wondering
Whether we need to take a bit of a breather.
It's a lot to take in
He's thinking we could go out into the foyer for a comfort break
But then he notices that a few of you
Are clustered around a picture
That's caught your attention.

In this picture
A long line of people queue in the street with their pets
Cats and dogs in baskets, cradled in the arms of their owners
Or sitting patiently on the pavement.
You read the caption:
'In May 1942 Jewish people were banned from owning pets.
They were ordered to deliver their animals to collection points by May 20th for euthanising.'
Some of you know what euthanising means
Some of you don't
But you can guess.
You feel outraged
You feel disgusted
On my behalf
You radiate a furious magenta
You reach for me
You say
No!

30   The Last Picture

Softly
One of you covers my eyes
You say
Don't look, Sam.
Don't think about it.

I'm trying to imagine for a moment
That I am not Sam
The beloved Year 9 dog
On the class trip to the museum
I am a dog in the city of Prague, in May 1942.
A fancy breed
Go on then
A pedigree.
A poodle, perhaps.
Perhaps my owner is an elderly lady
Elegant
Well to do
She keeps me clean and well groomed
I'm her pride and joy.
She shivers in the frosty morning air.
When she got the letter
She tried to turn me lose onto the street
To give me a fighting chance
But I refused to budge
I just sat on the doorstep all night
She couldn't make me understand.
An official steps outside the building and surveys the line
Does a quick calculation of the day's workload.
The people in the queue are trying to stay calm
For the sake of their animals
Because animals can pick up on human emotions
As you know
But as hard as they try to keep their feelings buried
It doesn't work
And an animal howl
Passes down the line
An otherworldly, haunting sound

Perhaps passers-by turn for a moment
Stopped for a second in the business of their day.
I try hard to imagine
The elderly lady
Drawing her coat around me
Choking back tears
I'm trying to imagine
Looking up into her face
Giving her chin a little lick
But I can't
I can't imagine it
Sorry
I just can't do it.
You will have to do it for me.

I am Sam
And you are the class of Year 9 schoolchildren.
Sir is saying:
It's time we had a little breather I think
And he leads you out into the foyer.
You sit quietly on the benches
Just outside the exhibition
Lost in your own thoughts.
Some of you take out your phones to play games
Or check your messages
It's fine for you to do that for a minute
Sir thinks.
He's wondering how it's going
It's hard to tell what you're thinking
How you're feeling
Everyone's going to react differently he supposes.
He's been surprised to see
Some members of the public wander through the exhibition quite casually
Making jokes
Gossiping
Or planning what they're going to eat later
But then again

Isn't that kind of like the way we all go through life?
Walking through blasted landscapes
With our eyes averted
Talking about dinner and the crap we've been watching on TV?
Sir scans your faces
Does a quick mental head count
It's such a huge responsibility being a teacher
But it's just something he always knew he wanted to do.
There's some music playing in the foyer
A piano sonata
Sir recognises it
He knows this one
This composer
The Nazis said his music was degenerate
Anti German
They pulled down his statue in Leipzig
Banned his music
It was played in listening booths in an exhibition
As an example of diseased, unhealthy art
Sir thinks he should tell you about this
But he can't quite get up the energy
Why does everything have to be a fucking lesson
A teachable moment
It's exhausting
Why not let you sit there peacefully for a minute
Bathed in the sunlight coming in from the windows in the high vaulted ceiling of the museum
Some of you resting your heads on each other's shoulders
The dog at your feet
Like some kind of sacred painting.

Music plays: A Mendelssohn piano sonata.

You are you.
You are sitting in the theatre
We are having a little breather.
Please feel free to stretch your legs

Take out your phones if you need to
Make sure everything's okay with the babysitter
Check in with a loved one
Or anything like that.

Music fades out.

Is everyone here?

We're going to carry on now.
Thank you.

A quick head count.

You are the class of Year 9 schoolchildren
We are in the foyer of a museum
Sir is getting you up on your feet
Telling you it's time
Time to gather your belongings
Time to go
Back in.
I am Sam your support dog
I am still with you
Remember
I am always by your side.

In this picture
A largish one
About the size of the big atlas that Sir keeps on his desk
A group of men and women
Dozens, maybe hundreds
Are gathered on a station platform.
Their arms are raised in farewell
They are waving goodbye to a departing train
Which is taking away their children.
They have their backs to us
We cannot see the expression on their faces.

34   The Last Picture

For a moment
You are not yourselves in the theatre
Or the schoolchildren in the museum.
You are the mothers and fathers
On that train platform
In the small hours of a cold, dark morning.
It hasn't been easy
To get your children on the transport
It's been the hardest decision of your life
But you think
You hope
You are doing the right thing
It feels like the only thing possible.
You have tried
For the sake of your children
To make it sound like a holiday
It will be an exciting adventure
A thrilling journey
England will be wonderful, children!
You will ride horses
Play cricket
And eat Victoria sponge cake
In gardens smothered with roses
And soon
Soon
Although you cannot say when
We will be together again.

You have carefully packed the one permitted suitcase per child
With their best clothes
Their favourite toys
And plenty of food.
You have been ordered to bring your children to the station in the night
So that the general public
Won't have to witness what is happening.
You have been given instructions

The Last Picture

Not to cry
To contain your emotions
Failure to do so might jeopardise the whole operation
And will not be tolerated.
You hug your children tightly
Press your faces into theirs
Breathe in the smell of them
Never in your life have you been required to muster
Such self control
Such strength of heart
As at this moment.
For one of you
One of the mothers
It's too much.
When it comes down to it
You can't go through with it
Can't part from your daughter
The two of you are hustled out of the station by a policeman
We don't know what will become of you both.
The rest of you watch
As finally the train pulls away
You keep waving long after it's out of sight.

You are the class of Year 9 schoolchildren
You are still looking at the picture
And Sir is telling you that most
Perhaps all
Of these parents
Never saw their children again.
The air around you is strip-light white.

Some of you are asking
How much more there is
How much more Sir
Of the exhibition?
There's a fair bit more to come
He says
It's very important that we see the whole thing

36   The Last Picture

That we look at all the pictures
It's our duty
Do you understand?

You don't really like it when Sir gets all stern like this
It makes you feel like you should feel guilty or something
Like you've done something wrong
Which you haven't
(Apart from pulling a moonie on the bus which Sir didn't even see)
Some of you are thinking
I mean I don't really get why it's my *duty*
This all happened a long time ago
In another country
I wasn't there
I wasn't alive even
I'm just a kid
And I'm not even supposed to be here
I'm only thirteen.
One of you starts texting your mum:
Mum I don't like this trip it's making me
(Crying face emoji)
But you have to put your phone away
Before you can send the message
Because Sir is already moving you along to the next picture.

Sir is getting anxious
A little impatient
We need to get round the whole exhibition
Before the bus is due to leave
He snatches my lead out of your hands
And pulls me forward
It's not very professional I'll admit it
But I let out a little yelp of surprise
Other people
The general public
Turn and look
Someone tuts

They read the words on my harness
And they think to themselves
This is no place for children
Who need emotional support.

But we must keep going
Because Sir is saying
Do you know what a ghetto is?

You are a class of Year 9 schoolchildren.
You're listening to your teacher read out some information:
'In November 1940 all Jewish people in Warsaw had to
relocate to the ghetto
After which it was sealed.
Living conditions in the ghetto were extremely hard . . .'
You drift along
Half listening
Half looking
A series of pictures of street scenes hangs on the wall
A man selling shrivelled vegetables
Another man selling bread
A woman serving coffee from a battered pot
A group of men and children posing with a dog
(Look, Sam!)
People begging with their children
Tiny twin girls with stick thin legs
There is one picture
That one of you just can't get over
A young boy
Cheerful looking
Relatively healthy
Manning a little kiosk
Selling armbands with the star of David.
You know about the armbands
Sir told you
How people were forced to wear them
To identify themselves
How humiliating

38 The Last Picture

How dehumanising it was.
And now here is this boy
Selling them from a stall
Like you might sell
Stamps
Or umbrellas
Or chewing gum
Life's little necessities.
You can't really explain why this picture shocks you
More than the ones of the starving people collapsed on the pavement
Or the group being marched down the street with their hands above their heads
And guns at their backs
You want to say something
To ask a question
But you don't know what that question could possibly be.
So you just come and stand near me
A halo of furious violet
And bury your face in my fur.

You are the class of Year 9 schoolchildren in the museum.
I am Sam, your emotional support dog.
We are moving into the next room of the exhibition.
In this room
The walls are covered with huge pictures
Of a forest
It's a moving picture
And you notice
That the branches of the evergreens
Are swaying gently
And the shapes of small birds
Flit from tree to tree.
The colours
The dark greens of the foliage
And the deep blues of the shadows
Are a relief
After all those black and white pictures.

The Last Picture

Wouldn't it be nice
To take a walk through the forest
To smell the damp earth
To weave in and out of the shafts of sunlight that pierce the canopy
To feel peaceful?
To chase the squirrels
Roll in the pine needles
Bury my nose in the soft moss?
It reminds you of the nature walks
That Sir takes us on sometimes
We haven't done that in a while
Maybe we could do it again soon
Before the end of term?
You are about to ask Sir that very question
But then
The picture changes.
You are still the class of Year 9 schoolchildren
I am still Sam the dog
But now
Projected on the wall
Is a coastal vista
We're surrounded by golden sand dunes
The waves rolling in towards us
The rhythmic suck and sigh
Perhaps we could go to the beach together
Wouldn't that be great
I could bark at seagulls
And we could paddle in the fresh cold water.

You wonder at first
If this is some kind of chillout room
A place to clear your head
To release your held breath

But then you notice the fourth wall
The one behind you
A blank one covered with pictures.

40 The Last Picture

These pictures are really small
The size of boxes of paracetamol
You can't see what's happening in them
Unless you get really close
Unless you really choose to look.
Sir is telling you about a thing called the Einsatzgruppen
(The 'special action groups')
(The 'mobile killing units')
(The 'paramilitary death squads')
That were responsible for the mass shootings
Of millions of civilians
Across German-occupied Europe.
They were assisted by local collaborators
Who identified Jews or other 'undesirables'
And

Sir stops reading the information
And studies the pictures intently

You move forward to look
Sir hesitates for a moment
He says
No one has to look at these if they don't want to

You are a class of Year 9 schoolchildren in a museum
Your have just been told
In a roundabout way
Not to look
So you lean in closer
To look.

Perhaps at first your eyes skitter over these pictures.
There are a lot of them
And it's hard to take in
Men being dragged through the streets
A woman in her underwear, running towards the camera
Her mouth stretched wide
A little girl kneeling on the pavement screaming

A woman clutching a toddler to her chest as a man behind her aims a gun at her head
A line of naked people standing at the edge of a pit in a forest clearing
It's hard to see it properly
It's hard to believe your eyes.

The colour in the room is as red as an open heart.

Let's remember for a moment
That we are all in the theatre together
In 2026
That we are imagining together
And that I
Sam
Am holding the emotion in the room.

I need to do a head count.

A head count.

It's okay
We're all still together.
Let's take a closer look
At one of these small pictures.
This is a picture of a group of people on a beach.
Five people are clearly visible in the picture.
From the light, it looks like it could be morning
It looks chilly
The wind is lifting their hair
And in the top right hand corner of the picture
You can see the sea
The waves being whipped into lines of frothy little peaks.
The people are walking across a dune
You can see the sand under their bare feet
And the clumps of sea grass behind them
The beach stretching away into the distance.
If you Google the place:

42 The Last Picture

(Skede beach, Latvia)
'Most beautiful beaches in Latvia'
Comes up in the search bar
And you can see how it could be beautiful
A lovely place to lie in the sun
Roll down the dunes
Leap over the waves.
In this picture
The group of five
Women and children
Walk towards the right of the frame
One of the boys is in his shirt and underpants
He has pulled his sleeves down over his hands
As you look at this boy
Some of you unconsciously pull your own sleeves
Protectively over your hands
It's something you do sometimes
When you're feeling nervous or unsure.

The woman at the back of the group
Carries a baby
One year old, perhaps
We can clearly see the baby's face
Some of you are thinking
That the baby looks familiar
A bit like your own baby sister
Or your cousin's kid
But then again
All babies look kind of similar, don't they?
Because after all
We all start off in this world
Somehow the same.
Towards the front of the group
There is a little girl
Six or seven maybe
She is hiding her face against the woman behind her
The woman who could be her mother
Or her sister

The Last Picture   43

Because the caption tells us
That this group of people are a family.
Perhaps they have visited this beach many times
On holidays or days off
Played and swum here
Or perhaps this is an unfamiliar place.
Perhaps
When they were arrested and taken from their homes last night
They were driven a long way
To a place they've never been before
We cannot know for sure.
At the front of the family group
Is a boy
He looks about your age
Or a bit younger
Twelve, maybe
His hands are bunched deep in his trouser pockets
He is looking at something to the right of us
Over our shoulders
Out of the frame of the picture.
The captions says that the boy is grimacing
At the sight
Of the people who have gone before him onto the dunes
And who are standing at the edge of a huge pit
Waiting to be shot.
You don't know how you would describe the expression on the boy's face.
Probably not as a grimace.
The dictionary definition of grimace is:
'A facial expression usually of disgust, disapproval or pain.'
The people who wrote this caption
Must have thought very hard about how to describe his expression
The expression of this boy who is about to be murdered along with his family.
They must have discussed and debated it
Spent many hours studying the picture

44   The Last Picture

Trying to find the right words
And ultimately knowing that any word
All words
Will fall short.

You are a child in Year 9
You are in a museum
Looking at this picture
You look very closely at the boy's face
He's a boy with short hair
Like most boys have
He could be any boy
He could be your brother
He could be you.
You put your face right up to his
So it is actually touching the picture
You have a vibrating outline of rose gold
You are trying to reach him
Through time
You are trying to say
I see you
I AM you.

Sir puts his hand on your shoulder
And pulls you back gently
He says
What are you doing?
You blush furiously
You start to try and explain
But the words don't come out right
Sir says
Come on now
Don't be silly
He says
Go and sit down over there.

You hate Sir sometimes
It's like he thinks you're stupid

Or weird
You shouldn't be on this dumb trip anyway
You're not fourteen yet and the sign said you weren't allowed
Sir could get into big trouble if you told someone
If you sent that text you started writing to your mum
So fuck him
You walk off into the next room
While everyone else is still standing around
Looking at those messed up pictures
You just want to be on your own.

Sir doesn't notice
That one of you has left the group
He should have done a head count
But he's too busy
Worrying about the time
About me acting kind of agitated
About what you're thinking
And thinking about what comes next
He can't remember now exactly what it said in the sensitive content guide
He suddenly wonders if he needs to prepare you somehow
But then
All the things we've been looking at so far
He's not sure whether you've been affected by it
He can't really see that you're reacting at all.

You are a thirteen year old child
You have broken away from your school group
You are on your own in the museum.
You've decided you'll head for the exit
You want to get out of this place.

You rush through the next room
Primrose filaments stream out behind you like sparkler trails
You scan the information signs
Words like
Deportations

The Last Picture

Escalation
Final solution.
You walk past a series of pictures of objects:
A teddy bear belonging to a boy who hid in a cupboard
A dress belonging to a girl who hid in a forest
A manhole cover from a ghetto in Poland
Where people tried to escape through the sewers.
There's a picture of a thing called a resettlement notice
It's a letter telling someone they're going to be sent away
There's a picture of a thing called a transport list
Every name neatly ticked off
You guess they must've all got transported then
There's a picture of a map of Europe
Covered in hundreds of red dots
And each dot is a place called a concentration camp.

The next room
Is all about trains
There is the sound of a train
There's a huge picture of some railway tracks
Stretching away to an unknown destination.
There's a picture of some train carriages
Not like the ones you've been on
These ones don't have windows
Or the normal kind of doors
Just a big wooden one that gets pulled across
And bolted from the outside
It makes you think of the freight trains
That speed through stations sometimes
With an announcement saying they're not stopping
Warning you to keep away from the platform edge
And making you wonder for a second
What's on board
And where it's going.
It never occurred to you
That a train like that
Could be carrying people.
But here is a picture

The Last Picture

Of people crowding one of those trains
Being counted and checked off
Packed in tight
Sealed up
A man in uniform raising his hand to signal to the driver
That we're ready to go
Ready to start the journey
To one of those red dots.

You know what a concentration camp is.
You're not ignorant.

You are a thirteen year old child
You are looking at a series of pictures in an exhibition.
The series is called
'Final moments'
In these pictures
A group of people
Mainly women and children
And some elderly men
Have just got off a train
They are waiting near the railway tracks.
Behind them you can see buildings
A bit like village halls
Or portacabins
You can see a high barbed wire fence
And a tall chimney
There's one picture
That you stop in front of
In this one
The people are sitting on the grass
In a clearing in a forest.
The old men are resting
The mothers are letting the children stretch their legs
Have a little bite of bread
And a drink of water.

48   The Last Picture

Just for a moment
You are not the thirteen year old schoolchild
Or the audience in the theatre
You are those people
Sitting in the forest grove
The sun shining down on your heads
Waiting.

This moment should be held for as long as feels right or possible.

We need to do a head count.

Back with the rest of the group
I am trying to tell Sir that we need to do a head count.
But Sir is not listening to me
He is asking you to look at the pictures
To try and understand what they mean.

Look at this one
He says.
It's a huge pile of toys
Teddy bears and dolls and toy cars and little wooden animals and bats and balls and yo-yos and tills for playing shops and building blocks and music boxes and even some Lego
You didn't know they had Lego back then
Sir is saying that
These were confiscated from children when they arrived at the camp
And a stray thought comes into your head
Probably inappropriate
But you can't help that
That Sir is always confiscating stuff off you
Sir is showing you the other pictures
Look
Mountains of clothes, shoes and jewellery
All sorted into separate piles
He is saying

The Last Picture

And of course, they never got it back.
Sir is saying
I know that some of these pictures are hard to look at
But it's important
You're the next generation
The future
You need to understand
Because history repeats itself
History is repeating itself
He's showing you other pictures.
He's saying:
This is a quarry where men were worked to death
This is the muster ground where families were broken up
Where children were torn from the arms of their parents
These are the line-ups where people were selected to live or die
This is where the prisoners were shaved and tattooed
This is the infirmary where people were experimented on
These are the barracks
The watchtowers
The gas chambers
The crematorium
Here are the beatings
The tortures
The death marches
This is the Final Solution.
Here is the wreckage
The rubble
The barbarities that erupt like rashes everywhere
Always
The perpetual devastation.
And in this moment
Sir sees clearly
He understands
That the only lesson
The surest truth
Is that all human beings
Are capable of terrible, unspeakable things

The Last Picture

There are no good people and bad people
There are only people
And somehow this darkness is a fundamental part of us

I'm sorry
Sir is suddenly saying
I'm sorry,
I'm sorry.

Sir is acting kind of strange
He's freaking you out
You ask him:
Are you okay Sir?

We need to do a head count!!

I jump up at Sir
I push my head against his legs
He takes a deep breath and says
Let's press on
We're almost there.
His aura is a fierce blaze of azure.

You are a class of Year 9 schoolchildren minus one
You are entering the last part of the exhibition.
In the room called
'Liberation'
We look at many different pictures
That somehow, to you
All become the same.
They are pictures of people who are barely alive
And people who are not alive
There are just so very very very many of them
They don't seem real
And even though you can't take your eyes off them
It's like something inside you has shut off.
You're not sure if you actually have or not,

But you feel like you've seen this all before
Many times.

Sir asks you if you are okay
And honestly
You are fine.
You can see the exit from here.

All of the colour has been drained from the room.

There's one final picture in the exhibition
That we're going to stop in front of.
It's a picture of a group of people
Well-dressed
As you would for a day out
Walking along a forest path
Lined with piles of corpses.
Some of the people are holding handkerchiefs over their noses
In the foreground there's a woman
Trying to shield the eyes of her two young children.
Sir explains
That these were the citizens
Of a town not far from a concentration camp
After the camp was liberated
They were forced to take a tour
To witness the things that had been happening
Just up the hill from where they lived
Through the forest
On the other side of a fence.
We cannot really know what they felt
Whether they were shocked
Ashamed
Disbelieving
What they knew or didn't know
What stories they told themselves
What they chose to see or not see

52   The Last Picture

But we can look at this picture
And try to imagine.

For just a moment
You are not the class of Year 9 schoolchildren
Or the audience in the theatre
You are the men and women
Walking along that forest path
In the picture.

This moment should be held for as long as possible or feels right.

You are a class of Year 9 schoolchildren
I am Sam the emotional support dog
And I am absolutely losing my shit in the museum
I am barking like crazy
I am howling like a coyote
I have lost all my self control
My professional bearing has crumbled
The colours are going crazy
Like one of those light up fidget spinners times a thousand
Like the last disco on earth
Orange blue indigo green red yellow pink
Violet bronze cardinal lilac topaz crimson citrine copper
Cobalt silver saffron slate fire heliotrope turquoise midnight neon
And I am shouting
HEAD COUNT
HEAD COUNT
HEAD COUNT!!!

And straight away
You surround me
You're telling me it's okay
That you're going to look after me
That we'll be going home soon.
Sir is shouting
What is wrong with that dog?

The Last Picture

What is it saying?
And you are telling Sir
That I need water
I need something to eat
I need to go to the toilet
That it's all been too much for me
That I'm asking to be taken home.
As if we could understand each other
As if we could really know what each other is feeling.

Sir is hustling us all out the exit
Because people are staring
We're making a scene.

You are a thirteen year old child
In a museum
You've been separated from your group for a while
And no one has noticed
Apart from me.

You made your own way through the rest of the exhibition.
In the end
You looked at every single picture.
For you
It was better to look at them on your own
Privately
Some of them frightened you
Some of them you didn't understand
A word ballooned in your mind
Sucking up all the air
And the word was
Why
Why
Why?

You came out of the exhibition
About ten minutes ago
And since then

54 The Last Picture

You've been sitting on the floor
Looking at photos on your phone
Pictures of your friends goofing around
Family holidays
Days out
Your pets
Silly things
Selfies
Stuff like that.

When we come out into the foyer
Everyone's distracted
Fumbling with their coats and bags
But I am Sam
The class emotional support dog
I see you
Yes!
I see you.
And when you quietly rejoin the group
As if you'd never been away
I stand close to you
And you cling onto me
As if for dear life.

Sir does a head count.
We all get back on the bus and set off home.

*

You are a class of Year 9 schoolchildren
And I am your dog.
In a field behind the car park of a motorway service station
We are running through the long grass
Chasing each other
Laughing hysterically.
It's an early summer evening
And everything is golden.
In the service station
Sir bought milkshakes for everyone

And he's wondering if you're having some kind of sugar rush
He forgot to check for allergies
And some of you are running with sticks
It makes him anxious
But he decides to trust
That everything will be okay.
He's done a head count
And yes
We are all here
We are still here
That's the main thing.
We can't say whether this expedition was a success
Hard to tell
What it made you think or feel
Perhaps you'll be able to talk about it in the days to come.
Sir reminds himself to tell you that he's proud of you,
For looking and listening
For paying attention.
He thinks
Perhaps
It went okay
Apart from the dog losing it
He probably won't take the dog on a trip like that again
Maybe the beach, before the end of summer term.

Sir watches us
Playing in the field in the evening sun.
The future is waiting for us
Full of possibilities
And promise
And for a moment
We are all absolutely iridescent with hope
Sir takes a picture on his phone
To hold onto that feeling

And this is the last picture that we will see.

56 The Last Picture

You are the audience
We are in the theatre together
I have counted
All ___ of us
And we are all still here.

The colours in the room are indescribable.

End.

Discover. Read. Listen. Watch.

A NEW WAY TO ENGAGE WITH PLAYS

This award-winning digital library features over 3,000 playtexts, 400 audio plays, 300 hours of video and 360 scholarly books.

Playtexts published by Methuen Drama, The Arden Shakespeare, Faber & Faber, Playwrights Canada Press, Aurora Metro Books and Nick Hern Books.

Audio Plays from L.A. Theatre Works featuring classic and modern works from the oeuvres of leading American playwrights.

Video collections including films of live performances from the RSC, The Globe and The National Theatre, as well as acting masterclasses and BBC feature films and documentaries.

FIND OUT MORE:
www.dramaonlinelibrary.com • @dramaonlinelib

Methuen Drama Modern Plays

include

Bola Agbaje
Ayad Akhtar
Edward Albee
Jean Anouilh
John Arden
Peter Barnes
Clare Barron
Sebastian Barry
Alistair Beaton
Brendan Behan
Edward Bond
William Boyd
Bertolt Brecht
Howard Brenton
Amelia Bullmore
Anthony Burgess
Leo Butler
Jim Cartwright
Lolita Chakrabarti
Caryl Churchill
Lucinda Coxon
Tim Crouch
Shelagh Delaney
Ishy Din
Claire Dowie
David Edgar
David Eldridge
Dario Fo
Michael Frayn
John Godber
James Graham
David Greig
John Guare
Lauren Gunderson
Peter Handke
David Harrower
Jonathan Harvey
Robert Holman
David Ireland
Sarah Kane

Barrie Keeffe
Jasmine Lee-Jones
Anders Lustgarten
Duncan Macmillan
David Mamet
Patrick Marber
Martin McDonagh
Alistair McDowall
Arthur Miller
Tom Murphy
Phyllis Nagy
Anthony Neilson
Peter Nichols
Ben Okri
Joe Orton
Vinay Patel
Joe Penhall
Luigi Pirandello
Stephen Poliakoff
Lucy Prebble
Peter Quilter
Mark Ravenhill
Philip Ridley
Willy Russell
Sam Shepard
Martin Sherman
Chris Shinn
Jackie Sibblies Drury
Wole Soyinka
Simon Stephens
Kae Tempest
Laura Wade
Anne Washburn
Timberlake Wertenbaker
Roy Williams
Snoo Wilson
Theatre Workshop
Frances Ya-Chu Cowhig
Benjamin Zephaniah

Methuen Drama Contemporary Dramatists

include

John Arden (two volumes)
Arden & D'Arcy
Peter Barnes (three volumes)
Sebastian Barry
Mike Bartlett
Clare Barron
Brad Birch
Dermot Bolger
Edward Bond (ten volumes)
Howard Brenton (two volumes)
Leo Butler (two volumes)
Richard Cameron
Jim Cartwright
Caryl Churchill (two volumes)
Complicite
Sarah Daniels (two volumes)
Nick Darke
David Edgar (three volumes)
David Eldridge (two volumes)
Ben Elton
Per Olov Enquist
Dario Fo (two volumes)
Michael Frayn (four volumes)
John Godber (four volumes)
Paul Godfrey
James Graham (two volumes)
David Greig
John Guare
Lee Hall (two volumes)
Katori Hall
Peter Handke
Jonathan Harvey (two volumes)
Iain Heggie
Israel Horovitz
Declan Hughes
Terry Johnson (three volumes)
Sarah Kane
Barrie Keeffe
Bernard-Marie Koltès (two volumes)
Franz Xaver Kroetz
Kwame Kwei-Armah
David Lan
Bryony Lavery
Deborah Levy
Doug Lucie

Alistair MacDowall
Sabrina Mahfouz
David Mamet (six volumes)
Patrick Marber
Martin McDonagh
Duncan McLean
David Mercer (two volumes)
Anthony Minghella (two volumes)
Rory Mullarkey
Tom Murphy (six volumes)
Phyllis Nagy
Anthony Neilson (three volumes)
Peter Nichol (two volumes)
Philip Osment
Gary Owen
Louise Page
Stewart Parker (two volumes)
Joe Penhall (two volumes)
Stephen Poliakoff (three volumes)
David Rabe (two volumes)
Mark Ravenhill (three volumes)
Christina Reid
Philip Ridley (two volumes)
Willy Russell
Eric-Emmanuel Schmitt
Ntozake Shange
Sam Shepard (two volumes)
Martin Sherman (two volumes)
Christopher Shinn (two volumes)
Joshua Sobel
Wole Soyinka (two volumes)
Simon Stephens (five volumes)
Shelagh Stephenson
David Storey (three volumes)
C. P. Taylor
Sue Townsend
Judy Upton (two volumes)
Michel Vinaver (two volumes)
Arnold Wesker (two volumes)
Peter Whelan
Michael Wilcox
Roy Williams (four volumes)
David Williamson
Snoo Wilson (two volumes)
David Wood (two volumes)
Victoria Wood

For a complete listing of
Methuen Drama titles, visit:
www.bloomsbury.com/drama

Follow us on X and keep up to date with
our news and publications
@MethuenDrama